AF292124

Maher Asaad Baker

Carnival of Sounds

ISBN Softcover: 978-3-384-44217-8

ISBN Hardback: 978-3-384-44218-5

ISBN E-Book: 978-3-384-44219-2

Cover image designed by Freepik

Contents

Introduction

Brazilian music is firmly believed to be one of the major components of the country's cultural and national image. As a result of colonialism, dead-end slavery, immigration and miscegenation of Indians, Africans and Europeans, Brazil has developed a highly complex rhythmic music that is rather unparalleled to any other on this planet. The pulse of Brazilian music is unique and its direction provides an international influence and it is a culture and an opinion.

It can, therefore, be argued that popular music was born with the indigenous communities in the Amazon and other regions. The bare foundational features of vocalization, movement, pacing, and percussion, exclusive of chants, rituals, and confident drumming laid down the rhythmic and the spiritual bearings. It is such musical knowledge in the form of an oral tradition that was passed from one generation to another.

This means that musical elements from Angola, Congo or maybe Mozambique were transferred to colony-era Brazil when millions of Africans were forced to be taken. Such things as call-and-response vocal singing, poly rhythmic metering and specific drum residues and blended with native tropes. These African retentions are thus enduring in Brazilian music to date as peace in the samba, and capoeira dance among others.

Regarding music, it varied from region to region because of the origin of the settlers, the climate of the new land, geographic conditions and interaction with other countries. The Northeast, which had a largely black phase, rose in the anthemic band and rhythmic songs and dance music. Region amazonense formed dances such as carimbó and cururu in which Indigenous, black, and European loan words were assimilated. They were displaced and replaced other European and Argentine styles like polka and chamamé became to spread to the southern Brazilian states.

International Bestselling Books and Rising of Large Popular Genres

In the twentieth century, some musical genres in Brazil became culturally popular and are now associated with the country. These include:

- Samba: Samba originated from Rio de Janeiro and is a fusion of African percussion and rhythm with dance and Portuguese vocal harmony. Samba is still Brazil's largest music export or the different rhythmic samba more especially that which is relatable to carnival.

- Bossa Nova: Developed in 1950, this is a refined mixture of the samba rhythm and the jazz harmony, which expresses the spirit of Rio de Janeiro in the best possible way. Some of the bossa nova hits included 'The Girl from Ipanema' which made it around the world-famous.

- Tropicália: Defined in the late 1960s by musicians such as Caetano Veloso and Gilberto Gil, it assimilated Brazilian traditional music and Rock and Roll with politics.

- MPB: This is a generic term used to describe a myriad of styles of music from Brazil from the 1960s onwards to some extent, which sought out both regional and other global trends to achieve pop elegance.

This brief introduction shows how geography, demography, immigration, and cultural borrowing defined the sound of Brazil. In the following sections, we look at the ways through which music is used in society in aspects such as; as a means of expressing identity, passing on information and showcasing culture.

While it is impossible to overestimate the importance of the regional dialects that show where the dwellers of the country come from, several musics separate cultural areas in Brazil. The baião rhythm which is embedded in the music paints a picture of the Northeast as a region devoid of vegetation. Chamame which is a dance based on polka takes one to the rural gaucho area in the South. There is a connection between Samba carioca rhythm and Rio beach party feeling which is associated with the city. These regional musical identities exist side by side within the range of the Brazil sounds.

The music of Brazil could be dated back to the time of slavery which resulted in injustice and as a result, people came up with musical forms of protest. The songs the African slaves sang in sync on the sugar plantations of America, were the call-and-response work songs through which they passed coded messages to each other. People disguised their unlawful fighting style while they were doing Capoeira and that is what they did. At present, and hip hop/rap artists in Brazil sing from the favela, which is a shanty town and inform as well as entertain, people about the social realities.

About the cultural relay, music retains languages, religion, history and traditions that globalization wants to erase. The communities of cultural identity in Brazil are practiced by folk songs Festival music and dances Samba school proceedings and folia de reis, rural procession. This is the sort of musical continuity that assists considerably in avoiding the processes of cultural flattening.

The official engagement in cultural diplomacy in the annals of music started in the 1940s with Carmen Miranda and has grown up to today's craze for Brazilian pop troupes. Samba dancers and bossa superstar João Gilberto are full of images that turn the exotic Rio into people's lives beyond national borders. Samba and bossa nova, for example, made Brazilian music associated with glamour as related to sunshine, sensualities as well and sports. This 'soft power' export cancels the pictures that people have of problems with social justice, corruption and crime rates in Brazil.

The two most important musical rhythms illustrate a process of merging populations in the context of Brazil – samba and bossa nova. One must, therefore, be aware that behind the term 'Brazilian music' hides numerous local patrimonies and practices that are as ethnogeographical as the national context in which they originated, informed by migration, slavery or trade and other forms of transfer. Through Music, there is a passage in a vehicular manner to cross cultural boundaries, it provides voice and continuity for the suppressed in language as well as offers a constant continuation of one's tradition from the ancient to the contemporary world. These numerous roles should provide clear evidence of the fact that music has a central position in the society of Brazilians. Other researchers repeatedly address how music does and shows class, race, sexual desire, history and other things in Brazil. This and other similar musical conversations will no doubt continue unabated throughout the years, decades and centuries to come and Brazil will continue to answer to their music through her stages, screens, recording studios and any corner that one might wish to turn a music eye to.

Indigenous Roots

We know almost nothing of the musical practices of the first people of Brazil, but their presence may still be faintly heard in the music of today's Brazil. Captivity and destruction of native European civilization and African slavery which was the adoption of aborigines as slaves was an attempt to wipe out indigenous culture in the country. While such modern researchers are in the pursuit of Brazil's early history, they are offered an opportunity to find out those first signs of music.

From the historical point of view, learning dates back to archeology, people inhabited the territory that is now Brazil about 12,000 years ago. These initial people migrated into the new world via Beringiam land bridge from Asia a region that saw them carry their music. This was a nomadic community that consisted of hunters and food gatherers who lived and traveled to regions depending on the availability of what is today referred to as foods in South America while carrying whatever little they possessed. There was also a need to ensure that musical instruments could easily be carried around, especially for those musicians who traveled a lot.

The indigenous Brazilian early music was drum and rattle percussion music. The first Brazilians fashioned drums from wood and animal hide for the strong bass beat which is so typical of most tribal dances. Small seed shakers and tubes have pebbles or hard seeds that produce other rhythms for dances and songs. Other common instruments were bear bones and wooden/animal bone/whistles and flutes and seashell horns that would serve as an amplification to loud vocal calls.

It would be logical to suggest that as early groups had been cultivating the plants by some 5000 BC and as they began to have denser and more settled in the village type of living then the musical diversification increased as well. Staple diet promoted the development of pottery and woodwind instruments which is a possibility with the sedentary groups rather than nomadic groups. Ceramic ocarinas and flutes have been uncovered in some archaeological sites of some ancient settlements; this means that settled life changed native music. Concerning the complex rattles and panpipes, the terracotta statuettes do as well. Consequently, the disparity in the instruments led to increased musical complexity adequate for documenting the changing aspects of cultures.

As in many indigenous cultures all over the world at that time, music had its place in the cultural, religious and even practical life of early Brazilians. Some of the songs and dances are very well synchronized with the feeling of the connected communities with their ideas and land. The culture was not built on the notion that music is a thing done in addition to everyday practice, but a way people interact with their world. It is essential to highlight that all these concepts ran through each stage of the ancient Brazilian societies and linked today's indigenous peoples to over 10 thousand years of their history.

The tribes that existed in Brazil had a way of passing information between the human beings and gods which was done through music. It's also possible to get familiar with the shaman's drum beat, with two flutes playing a single chorus in the song of plant and animal spirits opening the doors between two realities. Every tribe individual was producing music believing that song and instruments could express and accomplish ventures with spirits.

In this regard, music was incorporated into the concept of creation myths of cultures. In the myth of Tukano people of the upper Amazon, a flute player domesticated the animistic spirits of those beasts. When he drowned in the river the ability to play the music followed him into the water to be reproduced in the progeny. Other stories depict some songs that were made at the creation of the world and are full of tribalism. This is how the singing of the ageless tunes preserves the Spirits of times gone by through the oldest of rituals; the rituals.

While dancing in the healing and initiation, music sets the pace for dancing for the dancers could be admonished and warned by the spirits and gods. Soon, during the performance, the souls of dancers left their bodies and the members of the community started singing. The Bororo Indians of central Brazil would play flutes and, by doing so, they would get 'swallowed' by spirits, recreate the world and cure diseases. In lay terms, transcendental properties put a link between tribal awareness and another world in music.

Thus, singing was significant to extol the animals and plants, the fertility of the soils and so on. For instance, the Waura sang and others danced by planting manioc shoots using digging sticks to appease the spirit of the manioc root. Where harvest celebrations were held the Guaraní shamans used rainforest drumming to sanctify the tropical forests and thus mislead the spirits into preserving the resources. Implementations called for entities across domains so that an individual can engage in an exchange with the environment.

Traditional culture came very close to dying out completely after the Europeans particularly the Portuguese settled in America from about 1500 CE and thereafter the indigenous populations were evicted or exterminated or made into slaves. From the two to five million indigenous people of over a thousand tribes, it is estimated that only around 30,000 from roughly 275 tribes survive today, many in the most inaccessible and isolated regions which are all that is left. Some cultural practices that existed had disappeared because of genocide that had taken place for several centuries. However, recent efforts of the Brazilian government to assume responsibility for the crime of colonialism and return to native lands turned into new opportunities for cultural transformation and reconstruction.

In other words, out of the oppressive cultural animosity, there exists indigenous culture in the united culture of Brazil through fusion with other types of music. European and African immigrants though dominating the indigenous people's culture depict their culture through traditional folk songs and dances. For example, Capoeira-related circular indigenous dances with those of African origin. The martial art is an energetic musical dance that is performed on drums, and other percussive instruments including strings and vocals in celebration of the Brazilian theme. Other contemporary groups like Uakti evolved with Capoeira's idea by playing with indigenous flutes, bamboo drums and electronica in a postmodern fashion. These fusions allow the continuity of the traditions of earlier musical ideas.

Other hybrids including curryhop, invite even more global influences such as rock guitars jazz and hip-hop into indigenous song formations. Apart from the Indigenous people, musicians put synthesized drumming on techno beat or wooden acoustic recorders to keyboards and bass for a Brazilian psychedelic rock group. The law ensures that present-day persons get an opportunity to appreciate the works of the pre-Columbian indigenous peoples and assist the youths in appreciating native work.

Subsequently, in cultural discrimination and warring tribes, music provides hope. The Enawene Nawe people of about 5000 inhabitants who live in the areas of the Amazon have more often employed traditional yodeling as their means of expressing themselves. The whistled songs sung by the group members had a meaning that was necessary for daily life and ensured the continuity of the Enawene Nawe ethnicity. There are enjoyable songs one when two people are close and there are songs of hardship when the shadows have begun to envelop them. The cultural continuity of the Song may be carried on by Song, however, Song people may not necessarily want to be assimilated into the Han people's culture of modern China.

Thus, the first native intonations of the first Brazilian peoples survive today wherever artists allow indigenous thought patterns to express themselves through them. The ancient songs and hymns are rewound in the modern form, with modern voices, with modern instruments and in today's musical forms so that anyone who wants to listen can. Thus, that musical loom of the song weaves the past and the future together as long as the music goes unbroken to the future. Brazil in the present day still has native voices trying to inherit the musical tradition of its modern time which can be traced back to its pre-colonial era.

The African Influence

These people who came into this part of the world with their African drum and dance, cultural forms would inter-mingle and interact with indigenes as well as other European elements to recreate anew these new styles. Pain was transformed by people into samba and candomblé, ways of resistance and uniting against the oppressors. Afro-Brazilian music is an emotionally rich and colourful celebration of the souls who endured slavery and served as precursors to future generations of musical trends.

Portuguese were the first to bring Africans as slaves to Brazil to work in sugar cane plantations that began along the coastal area in the sixteenth century. It was in the subsequent three hundred hundred years that the process of continuous and continuing enslavement of different people including those unwillingly transported from West and Central Africa occurred. It was earlier pointed out that Yoruba, Fon, Bantu, Ewe and Kikongo people found themselves in an uneasy interaction with indigenes and Portuguese colonists in a situation that required negotiating and vocalizing in several Native and European languages.

This noise, therefore, laid down the foundation on which the development of an unusual musical culture was going to be based. While people were performing repetitive and rather monotonous physical labor, songs and chants in the African languages were sung. For instance, the Portuguese permitted the use of drums during festivals and in the course of the Catholic liturgies – circumstances where Africans could freely deploy their music within the rubric of colonial chic. The native cultures also targeted the soundscape too in the same extent, more especially in the rural areas of Quilombo runaway from slavery. Being in Brazil as enslaved people, but maintaining their identity these Africans could keep their music while living in a society that was determined to dehumanize the Africans.

Transporting Rhythms: This book of essays paints a picture of the rhythm of today's protests, making and unmaking, taking place in the United States in the first decade of the twenty-first century.

Against this backdrop is that polyrhythmic drum patterns as characterized by interlocking beats and calls and responses supported the melodies that were at the centre of African music. The people who were enslaved took these musical forms and, having very limited resources in terms of materials, created them all over again out of what they had to work with wood, gourds, bones, etc., and imagination. Yet it was a repeat of the African tradition but it was also transformed and adapted according to New World contexts.

Drums were of utmost importance for disseminating even news and you also understood magical incantations. These rhythms were performed alongside religious practices as well as other forms of ceremonial activities that formed part and parcel of the ancient peoples' existence. Slaves were organized in such a way that they could carry out these rebellions in many folds and this started to become dangerous in the eyes of Brazilian slaveholders. Indeed to suppress self-organization and eradicate unity, the ban was implemented nevertheless performers persisted and in the most creative ways managed to maintain the rhythm with the use of spoons, boxes, and stones. Thus the hope and the impulse of the rhythm stood at the center of the comfort and rebellion elicited.

Through the use of instruments that are developed from plant fibers and animal horns, string and wind instruments offer other voices aside from the polyphonic vocal which include the use of various languages. The richness of this movement supported attempts to prevent the assimilation of various African groups into a subordinate class. It enabled the continuation of community – and the hidden resistance – on the ship's hold, in cramped slave pens, and Maroon fortresses. Drum and the family of dance became the arteries that flowed with life for people who went through so many adversities.

mineral wealth and agriculture estates put in contact, and opposition and later on encounter, the societies of Africans, the indigenous and the Portuguese. In this process there were musical echoes In the years the culture brought into circulation fabulous music that interpreted a country of diverse people. Songs in the rural Africanized style and Tupi language and imagery that got to the larger society were these songs. In addition, the military regiments brought African drumming coupled with call-and-response vocals to their music alongside the Catholic church choir.

Urban house slaves on the other hand listened to instruments and authorized scores of formal compositions of the Europeans while improvising the compositions. The new peculiar form of lundu that characterized Rio de Janeiro in the 1800s was the mixture of African music with a European harmonic accompaniment and verses that expressed the liberty of slaves. Such kind of hybridity defined recent fusion processes of modern trends such as samba and bossa nova in the twentieth century.

The power structure of Brazil was in the process of changing around the late 19th century because of the abolition of slavery. After being set free, the African Brazilians relocated to the other rapidly growing towns and cities of the country in search of other black people as the environment became unfriendly. This climate paved the way for today's fragmented yet organic growing of Brazil's famous musical product, the samba. They helped to weld together descendants of enslaved people and made Brazil's first great popular song form.

Samba outlined the complex of musical multiformity spanning for centuries over the urban landscape using Afro-Brazilian spiritual rituals including the Candomble while at the same time involving those who desired spontaneous street dancing. It should also be understood how practitioners borrowed the concept of the polyrhythm and call of response, the improvisation and transformed the motifs of contemporary exile, diaspora and homesickness.

The tamborim tabaque, cuíca friction drum or the agogô double bell now provided color to the music in addition to the inherited skin drums or the stringed berimbau's. Tenement alleys and factories' way of life were condemned through the poem with the help of some Portuguese verse structures. The acts of major and minor played melodically with each other in kind of a dramatic rhetoric of the soul.

This re-telling of the past also narrated the present concerns and painted a future inclusion. Such a phenomenon of active disclosure of principal popular carnival spectacle then initiated the mass enfranchisement of samba's evolving repertoire throughout Brazil through the gender of radio besides migratory movements.

When Catholicism was established its rules compelled people to embrace the new religion Afro-Brazilian faiths including the candomblé continued to enjoy followers who worshipped in hiding. Music was notable in the reconstruction of vortexes of divine messages involving, dance and healing. Candomblé interacts with Yoruba orisha and Bantu inquices spirits by drumming, singing and dancing to recall these states, or in a more precise way to get into contact with the spirits.

Ternary beats lie at the origins of repetitive chorus chants aimed at Iemanjá or Exú in religious regard. Hora dancers point to one another as time ticks on with handshakers while animated entranced bonds with a gourd rattle. Call-and-response is used in devotional songs that become progressively more intense as cyclic patterns progress.

Although revelation to the public is safer, veneer resembled other Catholic musicals including processional marches or classical harmonies. However, at terreiros everyone disconnected from modernity, batá drums and traditional poly-rhythm took them back to Africa and/or native roots. This rich but tacit spiritual line continues to perform in defining Brazilian cultural experience and artistic point of view.

As far as slavery and the vices of the society that came with it were concerned, the nation had those imprints in their minds. But rich Afro-Brazilian music was derived from bitter bitter souring and expression of bitterness. The nostalgic longing in the oft' raw samba tunes, the mysterious practices hidden behind candomblé, and the dance that is the hallmark of life, all point towards creativity even when one is confined to a cage.

As audaciously keeping blatant and hidden musical links, thus oppressed the culturally Brazilian African-descent people also developed a liberating popular cultural stream in the Brazilian society. Their beats can be found beyond the sugar fields and senzala quarters and brought on the revolution in the music that was waiting. Taken internationally these have shaped all the subsequent generations of jazz, rock, funk, dance and pop the world over.

Today millions of people can testify that oppression was once experienced while having fun, samba dancing during the carnival in Rio or chanting candomblé to release their spirits. The descendants of black people translated chains into hope and culture in which roots grow freedom and family over and over. Its timeless rhythms ring in the decades as an artist's avenues of expressing custom and culture. Brazil resonates today with the synesthetic taste of the fruits that come out of displacement and presentation.

Portuguese Heritage

The rhythmic and harmonic rhythms of Brazilian music had the world on its feet. Brazilian music includes Samba, Bossa nova and Tropicalia sub-genres of music which can be attributed to African, indigenous and European influence. Of this one can say that the Portuguese left a strong imprint on Brazilian music. Portugal had direct colonial rule over Brazil for over three centuries and hence they could not fail to have a great impact on the country. Especially in popular rhythmic styles of Brazilian folk this influence was strongly revealed and stimulated the emergence of new subgenres of modinha and seresta.

Portugal started colonization of Brazil in the year 1500 and ended in 1822, during this time more than 700000 African slaves were transported to Brazil to work as slaves in sugar plantations. The Portuguese colonists also brought the music which their music evolved with influence from the indigenous people and Africans. Sad tunes mainly originated from Portugal and are called Fado and may be considered as a European import. Fado means fate and truly, it is a sad genre of music; It is performed as an individual sings and dances alone on stage like a flamenco. It began to develop with the poor and marginalized groups as a means of being able to express the kind of suffering that they have to endure. The novel type of the Brazilian fado is in harmony with the depressive nature of the parent genre some of them are sorrowful guitar and mourning voice. It is unclear whether fado existed in Brazil before the arrival of the Portuguese to the country since there is no documented history of fado in Brazil; However, data found show that fado became popular in Brazil at the beginning of the nineteenth century, specifically at 1820 in Rio de Janeiro and Sao Paulo main regions established by the Portuguese.

Apart from this popularized fado, the Portuguese introduced the Brazilians to other forms of folk dances such as the Chula and the vira – both are couple dances. Vira has the chorus section where the singers sing in a call/answer pattern in most cases. Chula involves poetic improvised verses and the performers used spoken words that were in fusion with six-eight beats. It is by that time that the old Portuguese styles began to be influenced with native rhythm and instruments in Brazil. The interaction of the continental and local cultures there thus came up with completely new styles of music.

The first of such a hybrid from the early colonial period is modinha which is a kind of sentimental song of love on European classical motifs. Modinha was born at the end of the 1700s from the Portuguese traditional vocal musical touches combined with the West African rhythmical interjections. The name perhaps has its origin from moda which is the Portuguese word that translates to fashion or style. The literal meaning of the term modinha may be translated as 'modern', that is, modinha songs were close in style to the most popular urban music of the first decades of the nineteenth century in Brazil. They are mostly related to love, for example, a love that has not been returned or the 'saudade' which was also traditional in most of the fado.

Modinha presents distinctively Portuguese elements: from the context of the harmonic-melodic language related to the classical tradition to the meaning of the romanticized exotic. However, it remains evident that with syncopated African rhythms, hand drums as well as call and response phrasing modinha was turned into something that could be described as otherworldly. This genre proved to be very successful and it began with Brazil and then went on to Portugal and spread to other colonies like Cape Verde or Goa, India thus evidencing the popularity of the mix of the two genres. Modinha was different from the portrayed society of colonial Brazil because it was not categorized by class; everyone from rich planters to farmhands, the black slaves, the newly freed Persons of color and the white-skinned laborers danced the modinha.

Another way in which the people of Portugal made their contribution to the music of Brazil was through Seresta which is another dance music. Coined in the 1800s, this tradition involves musicians visiting one house to the next and performing choros which is an instrumental for the guitar and singers. Serestas can happen randomly at the corners of the patios and other areas such as the squares. He and his band performers sing the scarcest lyrics defying the beauty of the guitar, romantic love as well and Brazilian landscapes.

Thus, regarding music, it is evident that choro is European in harmony and compositional techniques but its spirit is African and

Brazilian. That is why, Choro has elements of fast tempo and syncopation at the base of the cultures that joined together. It originated from the word chorar which implies crying, in consideration of this, this type of poetry is often depressing, and lyrical. Like fado, modinha and to some extent seresta the textual theme of the song in question will be saudade, longing and suffering. As such, while, it will not be fitting to assert that the Portuguese colonists have stamped a deep influence on the broad parameter of Brazilian folk music, it remains noticeable that the lyrical essence of modinha and seresta in Brazil has been colored with the colonists' imprint.

In addition to Catholic and colonial music, the gaucho's people were also introduced to Portuguese music as the country was one of the colonial masters of Brazil. In the Baroque period, there was a greater chance that Portuguese compositions or conductors would be able to get employment in those Royal Courts because they had been trained in the classical mode. They brought the values of the European upper classes to help produce clean sacred music and opera in large cities. Other Brazilian composers of the period include Jose Mauricio Nunes Garcia, who was also educated in European style, by master with Portuguese relation. To support the establishment of nationalist classical Brazilian music Nunes Garcia incorporated these continental models with Afro-Brazilian rhythms.

However, as opposed to the earlier endeavors of the Portuguese musicians, who played in the orchestra and theatres thus entertaining the aristocracy, the rhythms of the Brazilian Streets degraded the imported high culture into something they could barely recognize. Thus, the Africanization of various genres that happened through the slave diaspora was very significant in this process. When Africans incorporated folk styles for instance lundu they were far more energetic and grounded than the equivalent Portuguese folk styles.

Portugal also contributed pioneer instruments that were developed and incorporated in the country, namely Brazil. The cavaquinho is a small stringed instrument similar to the ukulele and it is believed that it has an Italian connection to the braguinha of Portugal. Another instrument, acoustic guitar, originated in Portugal and was popular in samba and choro. The cavaquinho from Brazil, on the other hand, has only four strings and does not have a wooden soundboard like the said instrument but instead, resembles something that produces a drum-like sound. It was thus the flexibility that characterized the use of Portuguese-derived instruments that became important in the fusion of Afro-Brazilian charity.

From blooming in colonial religious fields to inspiring the workers' imagination, Portuguese music left an immeasurable result in Brazil. But this transmission place not only in the Royal Palace but also in the public places, including the Square. These appropriations altered the directions that Portuguese traditions, such as lundu, fado, and modinha, would take: Africanized and Brazilianized The two terms: Africanized and Brazilianized were used interchangeably throughout the literature. Hence, culture change harbingered coloured and artistic existence as the social hierarchy established by colonial masters was brought to the knees.

Even though Musical Portuguese can be viewed as part of the Brazilian music stock, it can be spotted most actively in the framework of folk music. Even today the modinha is linked to modern Brazil it retains both the classical patterns of composition and the sentimental texts. As recent as today's singers such as Alcione and Zeca Baleiro artists are still negotiating pop modinha. In Fado, an outstanding singer named Ramiro Mussot played a role in the paradigm of guitar in Portugal as far as the process of folklorization is concerned. In the same manner, Mussot's conjunto regional demonstrates how fado is embraced differently in the large musical sphere in Brazil besides the social context.

Some other related genres include other forms of modinha, fado and lundu are also present in the structures and lyricism of its superior genre bossa nova and samba. Rock, pop and hip hop as well as other forms of music get a new lease of life in the hands of old colonial practices. The Armenian filmmaker made this group of Afro-Brazilian rap influential to pay tribute to this tradition with songs such as "Fado Oriental" fusing the Portuguese guitar and militant rhythms. To see that present-day colonizers' music styles are easily linked to styles that are centuries old, can look like an oxymoron and as if two different and unrelated musical genres are being connected. As such, even today the feeling of hybridity remains an important aspect of the Brazilian culture.

There is another field, musical education and commerce, in which Portuguese influence does seem to still linger seen in excerpt from the following features. As in Portugal, the academies of music in Brazil impart written-European music, and the sophisticated type, embracing European theories, regarded as being superior to the natural folk forms. In addition to the cooperation of Portuguese and Brazilian television channels in the framework of the organization of talent shows of musical types containing fado. This pop treatment of a working-class genre draws attention to the fact of the extensive domination of the Portuguese in almost all spheres of the musical industry in Brazil, from the high circles to the lower ones.

However, this aspect only goes halfway in explaining why songs that once topped charts internationally and belonged to the Brazilian music category of Bossa Nova have since stagnated at home and in favor of technical finesse over brute creativity. Even musical movements in general such as the Tropicalia of the 1970s dealt with this propensity. Both these avant-garde performers intentionally included 'primitive' and folk motifs coming from the periphery of the Brazilian culture to fight the prejudices of the educated elites.

But for matters of preservation or erections, one understands the necessity of institutional support especially since the genres such as modinha and fado seem to be fading away before both mass media. Grassroots movements do sustain traditional practices through festivals for instance the Rio de Janeiro festival of Seresta. Therefore, institutional actions have also disseminated genres to a newer population nationally and internationally but then the commercial side negates the spirit of genres.

Thus, the exchange of the Luso-Brazilian customs in music can be observed more as an active dialogue than as a passive action of colonization. However, it can be noted that conducting research in this direction is important because, even though the influence of the Portuguese styles dominated the official context, African and Brazilian inspiration continued to propagate the culture of struggle through the representation of the slave class. The above fusion was an endeavor to integrate society from below, several decades before the independence of the given country.

Today, Europe represents something different; instead of representing a victory, the European culture represents a victory of people's spirit over difficult moments in their history. Hybrid musical forms covenant of race and class in African and working-class agency becomes the cultural blossoming in the established colonial sociology. The end products became Brazil's musical miracle one which triumphed on the planet even as Portuguese political reign over the country waned. This joyous legacy is Brazil's sweetest payback and penitence.

Birth of Samba

Samba, as is well-known, has the status of the official musical accompaniment of Brazil. The melodies which get depicted are linked with Carnaval, passion, dancers, and percussion. However, the history of Samba will not start with the globalization and the commercialization process of the rich culture of Brazil. This lively and full-blooded style began appearing in the favelas of Rio de Janeiro at the end of the nineteenth century with Afro-mixtures of beats on European tools and preoccupations. Once considered as unliterary, as 'street' music, samba would eventually be catchy and represent the spirit of the whole country. It was also in harmony with other social transformations as the so-called 'voiceless' started looking for their rights. At present, some styles have already evolved from the traditional samba that also proven that fusion is possible with other type of music.

Samba has its origin in the early 1900s and belongs to the district of Rio de Janeiro most considered favelas. At this time the city was the capital of Brazil and was going through what may be difficult to term as a wave of urbanization. Ex-slaves started shifting to what could be deemed as suburban residential districts of Rio de Janeiro, known today as favelas. Here they were being packed into tenements with the very essence of the lack of employment, physical and verbal violence, pollution, and bigotry. This Afro-Brazilian demographic, in the long run, worked for the Brazilian culture in one of the finest ways possible, that is through art for the discriminated working multiracial community living in the central neighborhoods of Rio.

In these lively areas, a new category had appeared. It is a well-known fact that the core concepts of beats were inherited from dancing which was brought into Brazil through the slave trade several centuries ago. These were the Angolan samba with the syncopated drum patterns with call and response type of singing and other dance rhythms related to an Afro-Brazilian religious activity, such as the candomble. Then there were European instruments; used the Spanish guitar arrived with which Porto Alegre gave birth to early samba-which per se, possess the unmistakable sound of samba.

As for lyrics, they were to be as close, musically and thematically, to everyday life and struggles of authors of songs in the inclusive music as it was possible. In the early samba, the lyrics sung were in Portuguese and these emphasized themes like poverty, racism, police brutality and hope in music and religion. For example, in "Pelo Telefone" (On the Telephone), the samba of 1916 depicted police raids of clandestine gambling in the bugs in the inhabitants' quarter or; "Quem São Eles?" (Who are They?), the samba of 1929 depicted persecution by the oligarchs of Rio de Janeiro.

As for the instruments used in the earliest ensemble, one can say now that they played the combination of percussive instruments of both cultures. For example, the atabaque, an African drum is used to produce a low-pitched bass line and the ganzá, which are metal rattle instruments that maintain a constant ostinato figure. The Cuban instruments like the cavaquinho and the violão generated an acoustically typical samba rhythm of du-du-CHI, duo-du-CHI. But soon larger groups adopted horns and drums just like the surdo bass drums that characterize today's samba percussion.

This gentle samba was born and brewed for many years in the backstreets, houses, and bars of Rio de Janeiro before it got any kind of media notice. A decade later it was not until the 1930s that organizers started to then hire samba musicians to perform in municipal theatres and exclusive hotels for Brazilian society and foreign tourists. This attempt to promote samba as a style unique to the nation heightened with the establishment of the famous casas de shows in Rio including the Urca Casino.

In all the glitzy nightclubs, samba enjoyed a revival, maintaining the traditional songs but interlacing them with Western pop remnants such as ballroom dancing. The first samba singer, Carmen Miranda, who was famous for introducing samba to the world hence advertised samba across the world through Hollywood movies like 'That Night in Rio' (1941) where she danced and sang wearing stylish and colorful outfits with fruit headdresses. Although later accused of Orientalizing Brazil, Miranda's films and songs, introduced samba to different parts of the world.

At home, samba was further escalating its popularity in the 1940s as the Brazilian nation's dance. The bohemians who once turned their nose up at lower-class neighborhood samba started clapping in approval, genuine music of Brazilian ancestry, not inferior to classical music or European ballroom dances. This recognition paved the way for the rooting of samba at Brazil's grandest party.

Samba's crescendo came to pass in the grandiose show of the Carnaval of Rio de Janeiro. The concept of Carnaval has its roots among the colonial Brazilian Catholics borrowed from the pre-Lenten practices of the Old World. Boisterousness was understood as an element of parody where the subjugated classes got to reclaim their rights to social equity through the use of masks, costumes, fantasy, and role reversion.

As samba grew in popularity in 20th-century Brazil, Carnaval incorporated this music as its propulsive beat. The most engaging act of Carnaval was percussion groups and dancers in flashy costumes and huge, feathery headgear. Modern-day samba schools or Escolas de Samba now take months to prepare complex parades that involve hundreds of musicians, dancers and mobile floats. Today these events happen before the explosive audiences in the giant Sambódromo stadium complex in Rio inaugurated in 1984. Many more watch across the length and breadth of Brazil as well as across the globe. For those watching from outside of Brazil, Carnaval samba is the Brazil brand – a far cry from the rejected street dance.

Besides the richness of costumes and rhythmic movements, the advancing samba unveiled more complex social relations in Brazilian multicultural society. Samba's appearance showed how groups previously

excluded in the creation of national culture –
those who incorporated African elements into
their music, the lower classes, and the
outcasts – would claim their citizenship within
the twentieth-century nation. As samba
merged with soccer and coffee as global
icons, the music's growth meant Afro-
Brazilians shifting from the sidelines to the
main stage of Brazilianness. However, some
of them saw the transformation of samba as
the music for the masses and entertainment
as the loss of its protest and spiritual aspects.
Issues on commercialization or tradition
remain topical to the present day.

Samba also helped to assemble fight politics
during Brazil's military rule in the 20th century.
In the following decades during military rule
when repression grew, and demonstrations,
for example, were forbidden, persecution of
labor and student movements. Thus, the huge

public Carnival celebrations became sites of apparent challenge to the regime via satirical costumes and encoded song lyrics reflecting on inequality, police violence or infringement upon civil rights; As the Rio Carnival turned into an object of attention for international journalists, much people would watch subversive performances. So, even in the dictatorship period, this fighting samba spirit held protests.

Samba was born in the hills of Rio at some time during its incubation as a new 20th-century genre and sashayed through global circuits to infiltrate musical consciousnesses. Later samba rhythms combined with jazz verged towards bossa nova which took the world by storm in the 1950s and 60's following the films of Carmen Miranda. The likes of João Gilberto brought American and European fans hits such as the 1962 award-winning ditty "The Girl from Ipanema". This is the standard bossa nova song composed by Antônio Carlos Jobim, the genre's best-known composer; both in Portuguese and English versions it speaks about beaches of Rio de Janeiro and their sunbathing bikini-clad girls. Bossa nova fared so well precisely because it was this breezy extension of samba borrowing gracefully from outside influences.

The process was continued, over the years and decades, of blending samba with other styles. Sergio Mendes rooted samba-pop in the 1990s for layman artists. Some might argue that the updated globalized editions are not as honest as their more traditional versions. But to be certain, the syncretism in samba is only an echo of Afro-Brazilian lore rooted hundreds of years ago in basic human stuff, mixing different things to create something new. The roots of this cultural alchemy are mirrored in the creation of Samba a style developed from combinations made into Brazilian shantytowns of West African rhythms and European instruments around 1800.

Apart from commercial salons, people of samba heritage joined other countries through immigration, and the festivals as well as the cultural exchange programs also catapulted the element to new heights. Hence, the Brazilians have once again introduced the aspect of samba into the picture in the country of Japan. The latter is typical of modern large cities across Europe that have their own grand Carnaval parades, where samba schools are made up of expatriates. This is not true, even Colombian singer Shakira has some songs that feature this type of Brazilian music as her 'La La La...' that was performed at the 2014 FIFA World Cup and these numbers are even following the world music charts. Explaining samba's continued appeal in 2016 the Olympic Games in Rio de Janeiro saw samba play across many of the opening revelries which went viral to billions of spectators.

Of course, this must be the one that has advertised itself as a peculiarly Brazilian c dirty yet has gone global without integrating. Transforming from a cultural element of the slum districts of Rio De Janeiro, it evolved to become embraced by all classes and ultimately fully firmly entrenched as the Brazilian national identity and one of the new world music genres with its roots still in tradition, but yet constantly developing. Whether it is one performed in the devoted area called Sambódromo in Rio the one which takes place on the streets of Tokyo or London, or even in one of the concert halls, samba continues delivering the message that no matter how low the start, there are always melodies that can celebrate the language of the world which is music and joy.

Bossa Nova

The fifties of the twentieth century were the period of appearance of the new type of musical that inspired the people of Brazil and then the whole world. This led to the development of a new form of samba that included the aspect of jazz and this new samba was termed the 'bossa nova' in Portuguese literature; it translates to 'new wave'. Bossa nova originated in Rio de Janeiro in the 50s and 60s and the music style featured soft and rather elaborate harmonies with poetic lyrics as a reflection of the new Brazil in the context of post-WWII modernization. As a romantic and at the same time a post-modern musical genre that was born in the 1960s, bossa nova was a musical reflection of a new Brazilian subjectivity in the world. Even though the hits in the later period in Brazil diminished the influence of bossa nova remained global and its rhythmic imprint can be heard in the present-day pop, jazz, and lounge genres. Bossa Nova was also able to demonstrate how despite the incorporation of certain portions of Brazilian music into their products, the firm was able to come up with new cultural fusion that had not been seen before.

Bossa nova originated in the mid-to late-1950s in the Zona Sul of Rio de Janeiro, with a group of musicians, singers and composers: To name of few Brazilian composers, singers, poets and musicians are Antonio Carlos Jobim, Joào Gilberto, Vinicius de Moraes, and Baden Powell. Some of them were 'classic' musicians who wanted to incorporate the mixture of Brazilian roots with new jazz harmonies and tones. Thus the new generation of musicians in Brazil of this period was influenced by jazz either through contact with American musicians who visited Rio or through records. For instance, after establishing itself from samba whereby musicians such as Pixinguinha and samba singers of previous decades were prominent, bossa nova artists created a more fragile music style with rhythms and guitar and piano rather than loud drums.

Lyrically the first bossa nova moved on from versing most popular samba compositions to poetic lyrics; many of bossa nova's songs were written by Vinícius de Moraes. This was in line with the middle to upper-class standards of the founders of the movement. The compositions by Moraes and others are, in part, a return to the past and in part – to the new age, the modernization of Brazil, romanticized in the future, cosmopolitan. Meanwhile, the Post-Bossa Nova was a depiction of those fighting the process of modernization and tradition that were characteristic of Brazilian societies in early urban and industrializations under Juscelino Kubitschek's Plano de Metas' economic plan.

For the musical aspect, what characterized this style was the rhythm which is derived from samba-patterned percussion but plucked on guitars; this came to be called the 'bossa nova beat'. Despite earlier attempts at combining samba with canção the true pioneer in this field was Gilberto who sang in a whisper and whispering style and this was accompanied by the nylon string guitars and the plucked rhythm of canção. Another primary sub conveying was the use of accompanying synchronization and polyrhythmic playing between the guitar part and the bass line alongside the Brazilian instruments that include the pandeiro tambourine. Again, seventh and extended jazz chords included major and minors such as Cmaj7 and Cm7 within bossa nova arrangements including 7, ii7, iii7, IV7, I7, ii7, iii7, IV7 or I7.

Several first records were important to establish bossa nova, and to present it, to the Brazilian audience at the end of the decade of 1950. On one of Elizete Cardoso's albums entitled Canção do Amor Demais released in 1958, songs composed by the Jobim-Vinícius duo became synonymous with bossa nova, namely Chega de Saudade and Luciana The recording that signaled the arrival of bossa nova was João Gilberto's Chega de Saudade released in 1958, which had bossa nova's signature guitar-based s His guitar lines set the rhythm of bossa nova and his voicings presented a softer approach to singing where the voice did not forces the emotions through octave leaps or wave-like body movements but rather whispered.

These early records were followed by many more that progressed into the bossa nova style in the lead up to the 1960 era. Two albums in particular helped cement bossa nova's ascent: Antônio Carlos Jobim Elenco Brazil 1962 Surfboard 1963 Getz & Gilberto, Jazz Samba which was the first bossa nova recorded by other than Brazilians introduced the bossa to the American Jazz scene then Getz/Gilberto in 1964 which won the grammy award for the album of the year in the following year, 1965. Other Brazilian musicians who played a great role in the popularization of bossa nova are Sergio

Mendes in addition to Luiz Bonfá. Walter Silva being one of the radio deejays of Rio and musicians playing in the hotel circuit helped give 'bossa' its air time. Unlike the raw, street-level samba and jazz that characterized Coelho's modernist music, bossa nova's smoother, more melodic offering offended no one and was embraced by the burgeoning Brazilian middle classes; it did not even need to jump through media as it passed through them: it moved through them as an infection.

Bossa nova was the major revolution of the 1960s in the nuts and bolts of Brazilian popular music and has left the country's stamp or seal. It further elaborated already existing musical genres such as samba by mixing the effects of jazz into and aspects of classical music theory. This created a possibility for the beginning of the harmonic and melodic structure of the Brazilian music in the new harmonic and melodic opportunity. Bossa nova also served the purpose of taking Brazilian music to other parts of the world because it was more cosmopolitan; the mixture of American jazz was an opportunity for more Brazilian music to penetrate a more cosmopolitan market in the coming decades.

On the industry side, bossa nova institutionalized the recording, radio and television industries which supported popular Brazilian music. It encouraged even many more musicians and composers who were independent and wanted to set up their businesses and own tapes and release them through independent record companies. All this promoted an active fascinating music culture reaching the highest artistic activity. Besides music, they are aesthetics of the middle class in bossa nova and the visions of Brasil being the modern society corresponds to the national optimism of Kubitschek in the post-war years when Brazil was growing. Therefore, exclusively focusing on bossa nova as a movement, Brazilians proved that they were able to create brand-new styles out of imported ones, so bossa nova offered representation of the Brazilian in the 1960s.

First emerging in the early 1960s, bossa nova succeeded samba as the epitome of the cultural signifier in all spheres of life in Brazil including fashion and film. The popularity of bossa nova tunes blurred several cultural ways and aspects ranging from radio broadcasts to films and the like. Its words and visuals influenced movies and plays in Brazil during its reign. In theatre-based cities other than Rio de Janeiro, bossa nova's soft and romantic music altered other theatre cultures such as São Paulo and Brasília. The bossa nova lifestyle was also enthusiastically embraced by the youth and middle classes of Cariocas in particular linen suits or women's dresses which are reflective of the beach life in Ipanema.

Whereas at first bossa nova had been associated with the middle class, it very soon began to filter down to the working class. Bossa fanned out in the working class of Brazil starting with awareness via schools, excitement through dances, and identification through carnival societies. It could be due to its smooth beat and that laid the base for the development of new samba forms like the samba-jazz. Of more recent roots was the Brazilian funk, or funk carioca, which included the bossa nova beat in it also. Therefore, for more than six decades after the creation of bossa nova, it has been inserted in different levels of Brazilian music and society.

The great success that bossa nova gained on the international level during the 1960s secured its further development. Smitten by American jazz artists like Stan Getz and Charlie Byrd, Bossa Nova standardized itself to US and European jazz culture as well as pop, flukes like 'The Girl from Ipanema' notwithstanding. Thus, it allowed other Brazilian bossa artists to go and perform in other countries all over the world. Apart from selling as records, bossa nova was introduced into the international market through film and television; it was used in many motion pictures and with the kind of music most of the time adding a classy romantic feel to the scenes.

In the next decades, bossa nova persisted in other genres of music: adult contemporary, lounge and chillout music. Other Jazz musicians across the world also continued to record bossa standards. This style has been embraced in popular music with popular exponent Frank Sinatra and singers like Amy Winehouse and Madonna who all recorded bosses inspired tunes. Of late, new generations have been acquainted with bossa through contemporary giants like 'Mas Que Nada'. Originally developed as Brazilian music, bossa nova has become one of the international types of music which develops and produces new subgenres and styles known as samba soul and bossa electronica.

Bossa Nova itself in Brazil, although lost its popularity after the 1960s with the appearance of new trends such as Tropicália, samba-rock and MPB among others, remains popular with people of those founding fathers and most of the defining songs are still revered. There are a lot of compilations and box sets in response to the constant public request for the bossa repertoire which was developed by Jobim, Gilberto, and others. As the bossa nova standards, they continue to be reinterpreted by musicians of all the branches of Brazilian music for modern listeners. Recent examples include Marcos Valle's Estrelar and Seu Jorge's The Life Aquatic – Tribute to Björk, which confirm that bossa nova as an art form is by no means defunct in Brazil. Nonetheless, the old-fashioned bossa of the 1960s never turned trendy, but young Brazilian musicians kept on extending the bossa nova production.

Like jazz in the United States, bossa nova has been introduced as one of the Brazilian national music genres as it influenced the process of education and music art though it was initially an avant-garde movement that aimed at changing or revolutionizing approach to performance and production music, bossa nova was radical as it was integrated the Brazilian element into the style that was in harmony with the contemporary world and tradition of Brazil. Since it came to the world 60 years ago, bossa nova tunes that have samba and sweet-swinging rhythms are still rocking the entire world as one of the most symbolic products from Brazil. But bossa nova was much more than music: However, when boiling down to its essence, it was a symbol of a new face of Brazil in the international arena, a face of the progressive, emancipated, liberal, and globalized Brazil.

Tropicalia

Thus, the process that began in the late 1960s heralded a new style of art and culture in Brazil, including music in the combination of avant-garde psychedelic and Rock music of Europe and North America. Tropicalia or Tropicalismo was this movement that transformed the total face of Brazilian music and society. Tropicalia was from young Brazilian musicians who wished to modernize the Brazilian culture and challenge its populism as will be shown Tropicalia provoked fury through its camp and destructive nature. But it can be said that it defined the history of

Brazilian music in such a manner that its impact can still be traced in the present time.

Tropicalia was centered on the idea that within Brazil music has to evolve and innkeeper to art in other countries but which has to maintain its distinct Brazilian flavour. Tropicalista musicians were inspired by bossa nova and samba kinds alongside the several rock, electronic and avant-garde music that was being created on the international level. It was not enough for them to keep these various influences separate because they sought to assert these modes of consciousness-raising in aggressive provocative ways. The term 'Tropicalia' was suggestive of a tropical garden, which means that the new movement that the name was to present was not going to change the Brazilian sound now linked with the tropics.

Unlike bossa nova, which included clean, rhythmic, and smooth songs in their album, Tropicalia used loud guitar sounds, rough instruments, unconventional field instruments, and rough cuts between different musical genres. These experiments were always uncomfortable to the listeners. As regards lyrics, it could be pointed out that the songs discussed themes like poverty, dictatorship, isolation, and loss of identity and addressed those themes with irony. This reflected the tropicalistas' revolutionary philosophy: as an organized and conscious endeavor to confront the Portuguese-Brazilian society, culturally speaking, through the resort to intense radicalism.

What was left of Tropicalismo was two of its leading artists, Caetano Veloso and Gilberto

Gil. All of this together with Os Mutantes, Gal Costa, Tom Zé, Rogério Duprat, and Torquato Neto brought songs that awakened Brazilian pop music into the avant-garde. Nylon-string guitars and percussive instruments such as strings were electric and when it came to melodies and chord progression, these were substituted with stacatto and surrealist. Where songs like Veloso's "Alegria Alegria" and Gil's "Domingo no Parque" have the soft samba beat to be interrupted by out jams that mix rock n roll guitars with brass sections and stupid lyrics. Specifically, we see how Costa's version of Jorge Ben's "Que Pena" is an ideal example of the othering effect of Tropicalia. These astounding combinations are derived from the notion that Brazil only got into the counterculture of the 1960s in a disordered vogue.

Sarkis's artwork used on the album was provocative, an element that Tropicalia fully embodied as a reaction against the dictatorship. In his first album, back in 1968, Veloso was portrayed smiling and with a rather innocent look, with his hands gripping a large plastic ear implicitly telling everyone to "listen up. I recall having seen the covers of Os Mutantes albums where the band had very peculiar futuristic hair-dos and outfits which indicated to me that this was not the Brazilian pop of the classic tropicalia period. Even serious sociopolitical messages thus arrived with winking irony and pop art playfulness that labeled Tropicalia as a movement capable of stimulating both the brain and the buttocks.

Because of the political views and the critique of the conventional Brazilian culture, which Tropicalia represented, Tropicalia received a backlash in all layers of society. The left-wing music scene used to interpret these denotation elements as a sort of treasonous 'Americanization' process; simultaneously, the more conservative establishments observed in Tropicalia something ethnically other, rebellious. Government cultural regulators started doing research with a view of banning songs that they deemed as insulting Brazilian patriotism through lyrical content and that were being played by radio and television.

While their detention was brief, this, as momentary as it was, brought out the conflicts that Tropicalia raised between counter-cultural heroes/ youths and their boycotters. The youths in Brazil considered Veloso and Gil as revolutionary freedom fighters who were deprived of their freedom to change music. However, conservative bodies became even more emblematic of traditional cultures offended by tropicalista apostasy from gender, sexual, 'correct', and patriotic, Brazilian artistry.

However, and from the position of the revolutionary fringe, Tropicalia served a very important performance in eradicating partitions within Brazilian society and in the process, translating overseas pop tendencies. The kind of anger that it provoked only served to explain how much of those very attitudes it was entrenched. To disrupt such a mentality, Tropicalia was developed based on these three propositions. But it is known that the movement quickly disappeared in the first half of the 1970s when the Brazilian military junta began to crack down on political activism, Tropicalia has burst the lid on Brazilian music to tell the world that things can never be the same again.

In other words, even though Tropicalia as a phenomenon is rather short-lived, its nationalism in terms of dissolving distinctions between musical genres prepared Brazilian pop for the modern age of the global continuously relevant now. Jorge Ben was one of the musicians who combined soul and Afro-Brazilian rhythms in his work in the black Rio movement in Brazil early 1970s as in the tropicalia movement. In the 80s, punk and post-punk bands such as Titãs; Legião Urbana and Paralamas do Sucesso danced to middle-class youth's electric rock preferences and at the same time questioned Brazil's new politics.

Subsequently, bands like Planet Hemp use reggae, hip hop and hardcore punk to support marijuana legalization in opposition to conservatism. Other diverse artists including Seu Jorge, Curumin, CSS & Karol Conká are also developing into veteran performers of Brazilian music and there are two tropicalistas legends in the land, namely Caetano Veloso and Gilberto Gil who are currently releasing Albums which blend Brazilian music with hip hop, electronica and rock.

This constant overlapping of the domestic and the exotic is what defines the phase of Brazilian music after Tropicalia. Tropicália provoked a scandal in Brazilian society because they were imposing foreignness on native music through force. Later generations of people accepted this revolutionary teaching that change is possible if one is open. The music of Brazil no longer looks like it has a closed and self-sufficient environment. This revolt emancipated artistic freedom and multicultural communication as artistic procedures that now flourish because of the constant informatization of Brazilian pop in terms of the external world.

In this sense only, the sin of Tropicalia, which was mostly and primarily stylistic, had great and lasting impacts. It represented the imposition of the international counterculture to a Brazilian society that was rooted in tradition. The performative violence to the bodies as well as the vengeful reactions from the public endorsed major social issues occurring in art and politics –sexuality, nationality, and decency. For the young tropicalistas themselves, was it not joyous to be overthrown of these repressive status quos, the cultural warfare was a liberation – and personal, aesthetic.

But it seems that modern Brazil has little to do with the surrealistic Tropicalia, however, that movement has given birth to the avant-garde revolution that erased the definitive rules and opened the floodgate for boundless experimentation. Whereas it was possible to see Western rock as an imperialistic threat, Tropicalia offered it as a way of disenchanting tradition, so that Brazilian music could be fully celebrated as the authentic music of the tropical modern world. From the samba-funk to the once unthinkable politically charged hip-hop which is now actually part of Brazilian pop culture, which has now gone international. While the controversy went cold for years, the concept on which tropicalia thrived, defiance through mimicry, was there to continue Brazilian music's legacy into the realm of the entwined.

Carnival

Beautiful dancers, great costumes and carnival music concerts are associated with Carnival, particularly the one in Brazil. A fast tempo and drum and bass beats combined with even horn solos all get together to construct a fun feeling that even the worst dancers will not be able to withstand. Carnival and its sounds and rhythm represent the true Brazillian spirit of joy and is one of the most widely celebrated events in the country.

To be able to understand why there is music in the Carnival in Brazil one has to go back in time. The rowdiness associated with street fests and parades is connected to the European, Afro, and First Nations influence in colonial Brazil. The Carnival music of Brazil then developed the generations of distinct groups and traditions into what the music of Carnival in Brazil is now, which renews the spirit of the country as often as the Carnival season is held.

When the Portuguese colonizers began to transport a large number of African slaves to Brazil in the 16th century the oppressed brought with them their music and the beat of their native land. The slaves were forbidden to practice native religion as well as music and they were able to introduce some of the elements of the native religions in the Catholic call and Catholic feast of their masters making them go through.

However, the African use of rhythm and call and response singing, the use of polyrhythms from the use of percussive instruments and such traditions as samba processional dances became an essential part and parcel of colonial Brazil's festivities such as Carnival. As indicated in the study, the African musical identity featured more prominently at the commencement held in Yemen.

However, it is essential to point out that Indigenous Brazilian people have also made input to the development of Carnival music. Other native groups of the South American region that performed many festivals included the Tupinamba who sang and danced, used costumes, assumed characters and acted out plays that told stories. The Portuguese incorporated parts of these celebrations to their new Carnival outdoor events and masquerade dances.

It is noteworthy to state that slavery was abrogated in Brazil in the year 1888 and the liberated African persons inhabited the poor building known as the favela so that they could enunciate their African origin in an unadulterated manner. This led to the development, increase and diversification of the African-related musical structures like the samba.

Samba evolved up to the middle of the twentieth century adopting elements from the instrumentation of European-style marching bands and also the 'baião' rhythm from the Northeastern region of Brazil. In the thirties, the samba in its broader definition evolved into a dance that combined African rhythm and intonation with the instrumentation of the European brass band saxophones, trumpets, and bass drums to the others.

Samba held even more importance in the 1920s with the carnival blocos or what is called the escolas de samba (street clubs). Casa da Minha Terra (House of My Land) was established as a samba school in 1928; but as previously labeled in this text, Ismael Silva is known as the composer of the samba; moreover, Casa da Minha Terra is the first known school of samba.

The concept of Silva was to link Rio de Janeiro working-class neighborhood of African origin with Bahia through the musical unifier of samba. Other schools were established in the favelas and other poor regions in the Brazilian cities. They were key players in musical production and performance and at the same time provided a pride point for some of the otherwise marginalized citizens.

Samba schools organized competitions on the neighborhood level where they put into practice the rich costumes, the floats and movements as well as interesting new samba music into wonderful shows, in groups. It was a very formal way of bragging about their victory and also assisted in putting more emphasis on the dancing skills of their community, the samba.

Consequently, these contests played an organizational role that helped the formation of early Rio samba schools to the evolution of the Carnival samba parade presently seen. This rivalry never stops testing the creativity and innovation of Carnival celebrations all around Brazil part.

Therefore, as can be seen by the mid-twentieth century, samba, evolved into the national music of Brazil. Its incorporation in Rio de Janeiro huge Carnival parade event popularized samba as the sound of Brazil to the global community.

Today the word 'samba' is synonymous with Carnival and Brazilian culture. Such engaging rhythms lure about two million Carnival goers and travelers in Brazil annually. He comes to act and observe significant spectacles, as well as, due to affiliation to some school and friendly competition this carnival concept refers to the pre-Monday holiday before the Lent period.

Hence, the main fascination of Carnival seems to be based on the samba music which can be heard all around and with which everyone tries to entice their partners. Samba, songs are heard during the carnival, old and new ones, in any of the cities in Brazil when carnival is close at hand. Most of these popular ensembles get to be performed either as part of the samba school show or played by the bands during Carnival block parties all over the country during mass festivals.

However, the samba of Brazil has gone a step ahead and attained such great importance that September 13 is observed as National Samba Day. This event was held in honor of Dia da Samba which clearly shows how much the people of Brazil value this type of music. Taking music outside Brazil, there are numerous other music movements where akin to samba percussion, rhythm and dance have also been included in other evolutions.

It is to be noted that the Brazilians' samba beat has shaped global musical rhythms at the most basic level. They can be observed in such dances as the Cuban salsa or the Puerto Rican bomba into which samba percussion instruments or beating patterns are incorporated. Samba has been one of the major components of world music and other popular artists like Shakira & Rihanna are not reluctant to exhibit the samba step in their songs/ music clips.

MPB

MPH which started at the end of the fifties developed into a musical style in which all sorts of music were incorporated into responsibly socially conscious songs that recorded the political and social development of Brazil. Some authors argue that MPB was not only entertainment as was the case in other countries but was a voice, and music of the people of Brazil, in decades of authoritarianism and modernization processes. In addition to these cultural and political messages thus, the encouragement of musical styles that pioneered from Brazil transformed MPB into a cultural celebration of the Brazilian nation and protest against the repressive political system. From 'bossa nova' to 'Tropicalismo', MPB represents the art of artists that cannot be defunct from politics.

MPB has its origin with bossa nova, a music subgenre that was initiated around the 1950s as the project of a generation of new Brazilian musicians and composers like João Gilberto, Tom Jobim, Vinicius de Moraes and Baden Powell. These artists wanted to transform the routine Brazilian samba, mix it with the flavor of North American Jazz and pen in the elegance of French impressionism. The result was the tone and harmonic complication in the guitars and lyrics that depicted the hope and aspiration of the middle-class in Brazil during the presidency of Juscelino Kubitschek.

This new bourgeois culture was created in Rio de Janeiro and soon bossa nova became background music for the meeting places such as sidewalks cafes, apartments as well as the music studios of the writers and artists. Bossa nova was a postwar Brazil of elegance and worldliness and self-contemplated internationality while such musicality as is audacizable in the samba rhythm was inherent in this country. Songs such as "The Girl from Ipanema" started people to know this Brazilian music form in which people could feel so motivated and proud.

Looking at the political dimension, the period between the late 1950s and mid-1960s was slightly liberal and democratic for Brazil after the dictatorship of Getúlio Vargas. On the contrary, Kubitschek emphasized industrialization, the building of an ultra-modern new capital of Brazil, Brasilia and the liberal, creative society. However, the period of non-impeded political free market excess and simple embezzlement led to economic problems during his presidential term and contributed towards the 1964 military coup in Brazil.

In this volatile political climate of mid1960 bossa nova gradually evolved into a new formation that is known today as MPB or Popular Brazilian Music. It retained some harmonic and rhythmic relation to bossa nova but made a transition from being mostly non-ostensibly political to being highly political. Since the military regime came into power, freedom of speech and free media were curtailed and thus MPB songs depicted issues such as social prejudices, the plight of the poor and disadvantaged groups, loss of rights and suffering of vulnerable groups.

This new wave of MPB, composed of Caetano Veloso, Gilberto Gil, Chico Buarque, Edu Lobo, Milton Nascimento, Elis Regina, and Geraldo Vandré sang protest songs. Some songs were: The songs by Chico Buaque titled " Apesar de Você" (Despite You) which was r outspoken in its direct attack on authoritarian leaders; Gilberto Gil and Chico Buarque's " Cálice" (Chalice) which they used to sing against Censorship.

A welcoming place for Veloso and Gil was the home of Nara Leão, the "Muse of MPB;" moreover, it was in this singer's residence where Veloso, Gil and other future luminaries of that genre debuted with live performances; Leão's 1964 record Opinião assembled young composers with the seasoned singer Zé Keti who interpreted politically charged verses to samba and bossa nova beats. This record is considered as one of the oldest records of the MPB movement by many people out there in this world.

MPB then underwent a complete transformation during the later 60s and with Tropicalismo in Caetano Veloso, Gilberto Gil, Gal Costa, Tom Zé and Os Mutantes. This artistic counterculture was trying to subvert traditional forms of the art with help of elements of Brazilian music including samba and bossa nova in combination with psychedelic acid rock, concrete poetry experimental theatre and avant-garde art.

Still, in Apocalypses, lyrics as well as visuals, Tropicalism was portraying confusion and chaos in line with the Brazilian scenario. Lyrics tied rural underdevelopment notions to industrialization icons in a rather uncoordinated way and the songs hinged more on puns and metaphors to pass social-political messages beyond censorship. For instance, Veloso's song 'É Proibido Proibir' which was released in 1968 was also against censorship, but it addresses the fight gently without pointing fingers at the government.

While in terms of style, Tropicalismo with its electric guitar sequences and tape music was an electric shock against the background of bossa nova. This though was not undesigned – Tropicalist was meant to provoke Brazil's culture and politics out of dictatorship during the repressive military regime. The artists even titled their collaborative 1968 album Tropicália: In its basic level, it employs proverbs such as 'ou Panis et Circensis' that compare present-day Brazil with the 'bread and circus' of the Romans during political turbulence.

In response to this, Tropicalismo was met with resistance from the political realm together with some of the older bossa nova musicians who regarded Tropicalismo as a negative influence on Brazilian music. In 1969 however, the military regime ousted Veloso and Gil from Brazil and this can be considered the decline of Tropicalismo since the movement lost two of its most productive artists.

However, both the influence and the theme of Tropicalismo did not come to an end introducing new works both in Brazil and in other countries. It is also pertinent to note that Veloso and Gil's fusion of traditional music and culture with psychedelic rock also contributed to the formulation of the music genre that would much later on be referred to as 'world music'. Moreover, further evolvement of the Tropicalist aesthetics by other artists from Brazil in other new creative forms explains that It also discusses other trends such as 'Outlaw MPB' and ' Vanguarda MPB' as the subsequent developments

The political oppression in Brazil was one of its worst in the early 1970's during the military regime. Despite the censorship, there were negative impacts on composers, which came to detention, torture, exile or forced hiding or exile and the direct protest in MPB was reduced. Chico Buarque left for Italy in 1970 and stayed there until 1972 and Caetano Veloso and Gilberto Gil had not yet left England to finally return to Brazil in 1972.

Therefore, it can be concluded that the most visible art going on in Brazil was the dissemination of the government's propaganda. MPB began to stagnate and entered a phase called 'Festivist' MPB whereby artists started adopting the Brazilian folk musical rhythms and lyrics that would not get the artists into trouble with the censors. Names like Elis Regina, Maria Bethânia, Fagner and Belchior kept corresponding to the new beat of mainstream pop while sporadically masking their endorsement of government policies or simply luoxing survival moves.

One of such was Milton Nascimento, who was a composer and guitarist, but who evolved into singer/songwriter later on in this period. While the political message was not present overtly through the lyrics, Nascimento was very political in his music and songs such as

'Ponta de Areo' that are so sad, alone and desires, can be considered very political on their own. The song whose title translates to 'Crossing' released in 1972 is perhaps one of his most famous releases to date and it appears to tell the story of a journey and the challenges of such a journey in a country in turmoil. Likewise, the songs "Caçador de Mim" ("Hunter of Me") and "Nos Bailes da Vida" ("In Life's Dances") are written with a focus on the void in identity, role or any interpersonal connection during repression.

This is because after Geisel overthrew the authoritarian President Medici in 1974 his early years in office were called "abertura" (the opening) or "os anos verdes" (the green years). Later, some censorship policies were relaxed, thus admitting the return of rather blatant political statements and protests in MPB while enhancing creativity.

When Chico Buarque arrived in Brazil, he was ready to address the dictatorship where he could in his songs. His construction song "Acorda Amor" (Wake up, Love) from 1974 passed the censors as frivolous but people saw it as a call to wake up and fight for something different, Several of the songs were metaphorical protest songs such as Fado Tropical (Tropical Fate) a song inspired by the Portuguese Revolution of freedom from dictatorship in 1974 which Brazil never intervened.

He would also come up with one of his most contentious songs in 1978 – Calice (Chalice) which he penned with Gilberto Gil & Milton Nascimento where the latter features singing one of his verses; this is a protest song that criticized press censorship & the regime for not delivering on liberalization promises. This made it be sung as an anthem by student protests up to the gradual democratization process that later occurred in 1985.

MPB arrived from bossa nova's artful hope in pastoral folk remixes to Tropicalia's psychedelic pandemonium, taken to the political and social change till the last portion of the twentieth century. Concerning the people it has touched upon their suffering, their longing, their self-affirmation and even their critique of the society's injustice. The foundations of its rhythms and its melody are infused with a wonderful repertoire of both old and modern Brazilian tunes. MPB expelled some of the most talented artists in Brazil; with that, they took Brazilian music and art around the world. Some such as Chico Buarque, Caetano Veloso and Gilberto Gil made this only to become cultural moguls.

MPB is today one of the most important musical subgenres, born in Brazil and that keeps tradition in step with new ideas, tools, and change, as does the country. Moving away from protesting dictators, issues in MPB lyrics are more in tune with today's problems such as poverty, race, amazon's policies on development and corruption. However, MPB continues to have a strong sociopolitical impact on Brazil's sociocultural lives while still managing to stir up patriotism among the different generations of Brazilians. From the optimistic birth of bossa nova to the constantly evolving mixtures which include sertanejo-MPB or funk-MPB, this sort of Brazilian music stays true to the genre and answers the time, singing of dreams and rebellion.

Folk Traditions

Many of the most popular music of Brazil are located in the Northeast of Brazil. The popular dance form of the Northeastern folk styles is Forró and it is quite popular. Evaluated in the early part of the century, forró is commonly described as a model of the Euro-African-Brazilian genre that concentrates on such components as the random sound of a triangle and the sad melody of an accordion. It comes as a great shock to many to know that the lyrics of songs are very well written and based on the life of the poor people from the rural Northeast. The following are subgenres of Forró, namely; xote, baião, coco, rojão.

Principal forró artists are Luiz Gonzaga, the baião king, Dominguinhos and Trio Nordestino.

Specific to the northeast, other rustic beats including co co and en bolada also count as part of the region's repertoire. In Coco, participants sing in call and response while singing and drumming to circle dancing and in embolada, sangria is sung improvisational verses and is usually performed as a contest between two singers. The other elements that characterize repente musical battles include improvisation and the use of word games particularly in the urban areas of the Northeast. However, over the years repentismo has not only survived but remains popular and recognised as an important part of Northeast's culture.

The coastal state of Pernambuco has also contributed two unique Brazilian folk styles: Two of the most familiar of these are Frevo and maracatu. What is Frevo? Frevo is brass and percussion music with an energetic beat popular with the Carnaval street parade in Recife and Olinda. Frevo mixes African, Portuguese and Brazilian native music into a dance that cannot stop and leads to very energetic dancing. Maracatu is also a combination of African and Portuguese but they have merry groups and parade dancers and characters based on colonial Brazil. These two rhythms and dances frevo and maracatu seem to keep the identity as well as the pride of those belonging to the region Pernambuco during Carnaval.

The southeast city of Rio de Janeiro birthed two of Brazil's most famous musical exports: Dance and song. Emerging in Rio de

Janeiro's shantytowns in the early part of the twentieth century, samba is a highly charged combination of African beat and European harmony. Thus, disclosing a barely adorned body at the Sambodrome, or listening to samba tilting rhythm coming out of every bar and club in Rio de Janeiro, samba asserts carioca persona. Being slower in tempo and more improvised, choro instrumental also began in Rio with its roots in the cavaquinho strings and flutes with relations to the folk music of the Northeast region of the country. The samba and choro both began in Rio but unlike these two dances, it was able to go around the country and gain acceptance with everyone.

Another music genre that originated from Rio de Janeiro's neighborhoods during the 50s includes the mop and lush mellow song style referred to as bossa nova or the 'new wave'

Another renowned Brazilian music that has found market in the international market is the bossa nova. With the infusion of the samba rhythm with jazz harmonies and fine lyrics, early bossa nova artists such as Tom Jobim, Joao Gilberto and poet Vinicius de Moraes created a beautiful, rather sedentary form, which placed Brazilian music, into the international circuit. The romance of Rio's seafront is reflected in bossa nova most poignantly in Jobim's 'Girl from Ipanema' and in scores of other standards that Sinatra crooned, Ella Fitzgerald sang and musicians across the globe in every style subsequently recorded. While arising from the shores of Rio de Janeiro, the jazz-influenced sultriness of bossa nova was soon to provide a sound that was to epitomize Brazil for the outside world.

Bahia, one of the northeastern states of Brazil, with a mixed folk heritage most evidently during Carnaval in Salvador the state capital. Fast and lively are axé (ah-SHAY) bands and celebrations – during the non-stop partying. Axé incorporates the West African polyrhythmic percussion and it uses Caribbeans in it as it suits the Candomblé terreiro (worship centers). The biggest axé blocks, Filhos do Congo, singers Daniela Mercury, and Ivete Sangalo create a frenzy in thousands of costumed people of Bahia's folk. To the people of Bahia as well as tourists the axé and Carnaval rhythms are interpretations of the culture that has origins in Africa.

Within the context of música gaúcha, folk music of Brazil's southern region, assertions of pride in cowboy and ranching interceptor of Rio Grande do Sul transitioning Argentina and Uruguay. Using the Indigenous Tupi language, Spanish and Germanic, accordions, acoustic guitars and other regional instruments such as the Rebeca fiddle, gaúcha music creatively reminisces the pampas plains pastoral countryside creating sub-genres such as the Milonga, Chamamé, Vanerao and Chula/Tchula. In simple terms, the lyrical content of these rustic styles mostly portrays the romanticism of Gaúcho cowboys' capacity to survive on their own. Porto Alegre's Tchê music scene which is also called Tchê metal of rock, punk, metal, and Brazilian folk and roots also falls under subversive regional identity as well.

Regional cowboy identity also factors strongly in Brazil's popular version of country music: cowboy. This down-home 'country music was originated from the caipira folk of early twentieth century São Paulo and Mato Grosso do Sul states and was reclassified as pop music by singers like Sergio Reis. Intermingling elements derived from Bavarian polka, Mexican ranchera and guitar and accordion, which are instruments associated with country music, sertanejo relates stories of farming lifestyles in the Brazilian Deep South interior through various sub-genres to include cantoria music, música de raiz, sertanejo romantico and arrocha. Due to popular reception by the average Brazilian consumer, modern sertanejo and the associated music festival assist in promoting patriotic emotions regarding the basic Brazilian countryside even among the Gen Z growing up in big cities.

Although not as evident in a national commercial context, indigenous Brazilians continue to have rich musical practices that concern spirituality and ethnicity. More than 180 tribes of indigenous Brazilians live in the country; their culture differs significantly and often revolves around music, dance, and shamanism. Some of these groups include the

Guarani who are still struggling to protect their land for the sake of preserving their symbolic folk culture from the increasing agricultural activities in the Amazon and Mato Gross do Sul. Other tribes like the Maxakali in Minas Gerais continue harmonic chant and dance practices that are used to provide direction to tribes. People and tribes such as the Yawanawa are participating in international initiatives through new media aiming at creating awareness, and, thus, preserving endangered native cultural practices in comparatively secluded areas.

Several of the subgenres of Brazilian folk music are in danger of becoming lost or overwhelmed by contemporary trends. Bureaucratic and cultural organizations such as National Foundation of the Arts strives to preserve venerable regional music traditions through archival projects, musicological studies, youth education, and cultural sponsorship. Private organizations such as Forró no Quintal in Pernambuco provide live engagements to enhance the knowledge base and support Northeastern folk dances. Few musicians such as il Alceu Valença manage to balance between traditionalism and innovation by employing forró, coco, embolada and maracatu structures. Other fresher groups, for example, Tribo de Gonzaga or Orleans Street Band, also incorporate baião, originally from the Northeast, into modern music styles to appeal to the younger audience. Current maintenance efforts attempt to preserve Brazil's culturally diverse regional folklore for future generations.

But in Argentina, many musicians are also exploring new possibilities of music in blending with other kinds. Jovino Santos Neto for instance some artists assimilated folk styles with jazz, classical and experimental but the latter was done by pioneers like Egberto Gismonti who played the guitar. Other groups include Balkan Beat Box which is an electro-fusion band from Brazil-meets-Balkans that translates the traditional rhythms for the international audience. Other singers, like Marisa Monte, Seu Jorge, and Curumin include samba, forró, soul, and African rhythms within the indie pop genre to reinvigorate old musical genres. Some of the performances that can be considered as cross-genre include; Esperanza Spaulding's crossover album in 2016 with Milton Nascimento, a Brazilian musician. Such gradually progressive mergers chronologically substantiate that folk music not only preserves a tradition but also develops creativity in the folk music process in Brazil.

Almost all regions of Brazil have their type of regional folk music, from the western sertanejo to northeastern frevo beat, hence the regional folk music is the driving force of unity of the regions of the country. The economic modernization erases the contexts of the country that nurtured these genres, but continuous processes of conservation guarantee the Brazilian references inherent to the symbolic music. Through continuous cycles of continuity and addition, the traditional folk Brazilian music genres are as vital and variable signs that preserve the living traditions and transform into the modern trends that popularize the age-old paradigms of culture in the Brazilian skyline.

Contemporary Trends

The importance of music in the context of Brazilian culture and the nation's formation can be hardly overemphasized. Brazil has been the source of some of the most innovative forms of hybrid musical forms that conveyed the interactions of the Brazilian culture, starting with Samba and Bossa Nova and continuing with Tropicalia and Axé. Therefore, it is clear to say that although the new millennium has brought new forms of instruments and new rhythms Brazil is still Knave relevant in the new forms of music.

Originally originating in the suburbs of Rio de Janeiro in the 1980s, funk carioca is one of the most prominent modern music styles in Brazil. Miami bass electronic music with the influence of the African beats Samba rhythm and Portuguese rap-like vocals have been used in this energetic style of music. Funk carioca has a strong social protest in its lyrics: Some of the issues that are well depicted from themes it has include: poverty, injustice, sexuality and racism. That is why there are tendencies of integrating some features of funk carioca in pop music which marks that this genre is rather popular in Brazil and can influence famous world performers like Diplo. Due to its lyrics, Funk Carioca is a true and unique Brazilian genre coming from the favelas and has become a symbol of Rio.

Sertanejo is another type of country pop music that has its roots in Brazil folk music for rural people known as sertanejo. Sertanejo uses instruments typical for Brazilian country music such as accordion, triangle, acoustic guitar, and violin and are romantic, smooth and have been compared to the tunes of American pop-country music. Sertanejo of the last years and has included other rhythms such as arrocha, pagode, forro, and even electronic music which also indicates the enhancement of its trends. Nevertheless, some artists such as Michel Teló have introduced sertanejo into the international arena and sertanejo remains popular in Brazil.

MPB is an abbreviation for música popular brasileira and describes a more diverse pop music in Brazil which includes samba and bossa nova along with jazz, rock, funk and other foreign influences. The song is songs in distinct verses and accompanied by a mix of different music styles and can be said to be an example of MPB, which is the Brazilians for popular music. Currently, most singers signed to MPB labels are hybrids with some preserving the conventional modern techniques while others adopting other contemporary strategies such as Marisa Monte, Gal Costa or Seu Jorge. MPB remains to be political and socially conscious and this makes it a preference of artists in Brazil.

As evangelical Protestantism percentage has risen in Brazil, contemporary Christian music has been understood as a subgenre. By mixing secular styles like rock and roll, and hip hop/pop with religious messages of the bible, Brazilian gospel can attract many people to their concerts/recordings. In current religious music in Brazil, the Catholic Church has also produced singing priests including Marcelo Rossi. Religious music along with its charm has always been a part of Brazil and the contemporary Christian style support this assertion.

Axé is an animated pop music style that originated in Salvador mixing Samba, Reggae, Merengue, Forró, Maracatu and other Afro ROOTS. Axé is happy and cheerful, where the sound of the electric guitar predominates, which is inherent in Salvador Carnival. Axé was evolved by Olodum in the 1980s and later, other singers took it to other parts of the country such as Daniela Mercury and Ivete Sangalo. Axé songs are distinguished by a simple and active tempo and the texts have the feelings of joy and the encouragement of the Brazilian folklore. The vibrantly colored aesthetic is still a part of the fabrics that define Brazil's national music motif.

Brazil has a developed electronic music scene that was formed in the early 90-ties in major cities including Sao Paulo, Curitiba and Rio de Janeiro. Brazilian electronic is a blending of house music, techno, drum & bass and trance music together with Brazilian traditional music including bossa nova and afoxe. Today's electronic DJs and music producers such as Gui Boratto therefore can incorporate acoustic theories with contemporary practices. Other musical freaks that can be called experimental are such as the psychedelic tribal house group Deracine. An electronic music from Brazil demonstrates how musicians combine folklore with low bass.

Regarding the musical subjectivities that characterized each of them, all are the imprints of Brazil; but foreign influences have always infiltrated the diverse rhythms of the country.

Samba may have derived from West Africa but Brazil's music is being threatened by all quarters with rock and hip-hop enticing the world. It is noteworthy that most of the international subgenres like reggaeton, house, synth pop, metal, and others are used in Brazilian music but with a Brazilian twist.

Competing with state folklore, regional folklore in Brazil blends and crosses with each other. The other northeastern baião guitars accompanied by today's Brazilian country music harmonic accordions to come up with the sertanejo pop. Candomblé, the music from Afro-Brazilian religions intermingles with axé which is popular music. This is not true with Brazil which has an ethnomusicological very rich culture & Indigenous, African and European origins, that's why there are so many rhythms, instruments and styles that always produce new subgenres.

Therefore, while including global trends in its production, Brazilian music still respects regional core. In so doing, Rio de Janeiro musicians incorporate hip hop and funk into funk carioca a genre, which is peculiar to Fluminense. But funk carioca and its lyrics also move and are included in Lisbon's African-European musical hybrid. The markets for Brazilian music can go global but there will always be people who appreciate regional, religious and folk music. No fever global can liquefy the density of diversity that is in Brazilian music.

Orchestras enhanced their tonal colours through recording technologies and more especially through electric instruments while record manufacturing and record distribution standardized from the 1930s. These were samba and choro that gained popularity throughout the country by the influence of radio and records. Peculiarities of the modern digital world remain electrification's progressive impact and afford fusion genres, loud concerts, and electronic music.

However, at the same time, tradition is part and parcel of the threat posed by technology. Forró program-made and electronic forró as well as sertanejo are the musical styles that are ready to lose the instrument credibility for the program-made beats. Religious organizations may not appreciate livelier esoteric and special hymns or even MP3 recordings of the same. Challenges of piracy have still prevailed as a mystery for record labels and musicians. Problems of genre property and succession are relevant to the blackmail of international marketing.

Nonetheless, most of the performers embrace today's techniques in their performances. Axé stadium concerts thrill youth with dazzling stage performances, however, Carnival blocos recover the street samba of the tradition. What can be said is that he imposes Brazilian music on technology and customs. Through social platforms like YouTube and Spotify, the outreach happens all over the world; Music apps assist musicians in the preservation of heritage knowledge. Technology also makes music production more collective also evident in Criolo's use of Afro-Brazilian beliefs. It is therefore important to understand that, contrary to what was advocated whereby the digital age hampers live music events, it enlarges the inventory of Music Material along with Performance Strategies.

Modern technology acts as a go-between tradition and modernity because it even allows Brazilian music to be popular among a section of the community. Electro artists recreate and repost folklore recordings.

The interpretation of local identities in Brazil reflects one of the ways of enunciating future desires. Some evidence such as proposals for training traditional instruments in music points to the argument that youths retain an interest that globalization forces may combine. Religious cultures qualify modernity, to the degree, as in FLT studio renditions of centuries-old Afro-Brazilian compositions. Global giants bow to fabled petit Illinois markets thus emphasizing the lake depths of heritage music in parallel to the Broadway.

Specifically, the interconnectivity of the global system will make global interactions more mutual because of the expansion of globalization. Exposed as Japanese singers 'bossa nova' remixing the 1960s, K-pop and Latin trap remix Brazilian pop. Europe, Africa and the United States of America interact with the music makers of Brazil. Musical exchange is the logical progression of economic relations with the Middle East, Asia and Latin America. In this manner, Migration makes way to enrich national personalities with new conceptions for the native societies. Music also underlines change in the sense that when the number of voices increases, new concepts are postulated and therefore new rhythms or patterns of life emerge.

Some new prospective futures are possible and these avenues need to be protected for as much diversity as possible. The biggest danger here lies in what is known as a commodification of the scene. In its turn sertanejo music and gospel are likely to become an instrument of ideological propaganda or be included in piracy circuits. This is particularly so since genres such as pop are less fortunate and endangered and therefore need to be preserved through support in music education and culture. Musical activism confronts the oppressive power which seeks to silence victims and has the potential to invert injustice.

So, with having necessary technologies and state support, all the communities of Brazil can successfully develop in music. To sustain carnivalesque constituent and generic, ideological, and creator diversity must be invited. There is a brave cooperation in Brazil's sonic stew that defies the regimes of art production.

Whether it's the funk favela dancers or Sao Paulo ravers, the Brazilians are well known to embrace live music. They are based on a vast array of sources, provide constantly oscillating tones and tell of regional and ethnological fragmentation of the country. With the progress of one's technology, new genres re-establish good steady musical personas as there must be upkeep as well as progression. Thus, with appropriate supportive conditions, Brazilian music can continue making the world through music and at the same time paying traditional homage. Brazil will then keep pulsating abroad to beats that are classically its own and woven out from the tapestry of its people's dreams.

Disclaimer

Everything shared in this book should be considered as educational and informative in nature. The author and publisher shall not be responsible for any loss or damage suffered by any reader directly or indirectly through reading of, reliance on, and use of information that only the author and the publisher know at the time of writing this book.

Some of the suggestions given and the approaches recommended in the book may not be applicable to certain circumstances. The author and the publisher shall not be held responsible for any damages caused as a direct result of the use or non-use of the information presented in this book.

It is understood that readers should not rely on it for professional solicitations such as medical, legal, financial, and other related opinions. If any professional help is needed, then advice of a competent professional person should be taken.

The author and the publisher will not be held responsible for direct, indirect, special, or consequential damages or any other costs whatsoever arising from the use of the information present herein in this book.

About the Author

Maher Asaad Baker (In Arabic: ماهر أسعد بكر), is a Syrian musician, author, journalist, VFX & graphic artist, and director. He was born in Damascus in 1977. He grew up with a dream of being one of the most well-known artists in the world, and he has been working hard to achieve it ever since.

He started his career in 1997 when he was only 20 years old. He had a passion for technology and media, and he taught himself how to develop applications and websites. He also explored various types of media-creating paths, such as music production, graphic design, video editing, animation, and filmmaking. He was not satisfied with just being a consumer of media; he wanted to be a creator of media.

Reading was another source of inspiration for him. He was always surrounded by books as a child, thanks to his father's extensive library. He read books from different genres, topics, and perspectives. He read books for knowledge, for wisdom, for entertainment, for enlightenment. Reading stimulated his imagination and curiosity. Reading also developed his writing skills.

He did not start writing professionally until later in his life, as he was busy with other projects and pursuits. But when he did start writing, he proved himself to be a talented and prolific writer. He wrote articles for various newspapers and magazines on topics such as politics, culture, society, art, technology, and more. He wrote books that were informative and insightful. He wrote books that were creative and captivating. He wrote books that were best-selling and award-winning.

He is most known for his book "How I wrote a million Wikipedia articles", where he shares his experience of being one of the most prolific contributors to the online encyclopedia. He reveals his methods, techniques, strategies, and secrets of writing high-quality articles on any subject in record time. He also discusses the benefits and challenges of being a Wikipedia editor in the age of information overload.

He is also known for his novel "Becoming the man", where he tells the story of a young man who goes through a series of transformations in his life. The novel explores themes such as identity, masculinity, self-discovery, love, loss, and redemption. The novel is based on his journey to becoming who he is today.

Copyright © 2024 Maher Asaad Baker